Dynamic Solos for Snare Drum

By Brian Slawson

Table of Contents

Foreword 2

Explanation of Terms 2

1. Boots & Slippers 3

2. Knock, Knock, Who's There? 4

3. Right Away 5

4. Two Left On 6

5. Blues in Three 7

6. Calypso Hippo 8

7. Soft-Shoe Louie 9

8. Horseplay 10

9. Double Dippo, Dancing Hippo 12

10. Waltzing Brunhilda 13

11. Both Sides March 14

12. Grand Canyon 15

13. Jamtrak 16

14. Planet Roll 18

15. The Curious Count 19

16. Subdivider 20

17. Groove Trail 21

18. Uncle's Ant Farm 22

About the Author 24

Alfred's
PERCUSSION
PERFORMANCE SERIES

Alfred

Foreword

Dynamics are one of the greatest resources we have to help us convey expression in music. As soon as students understand that the most basic musical ideas can be transformed by the use of dynamics, they become an inherent part of their playing, much like reading simple rhythms and keeping a steady beat.

Dynamic Solos for Snare Drum contains a progressive variety of performance pieces, all designed to help enforce the recognition of dynamics, as well as attention to detail.

Here are some basic tips to help maximize results while using this text:

- Keep a steady beat at all times, and practice with a metronome.
- Soft does not mean slow, so maintain your intensity when playing softly.
- Loud (or accented) does not mean fast, so stay relaxed when playing loudly.
- Establish a sense of meter by counting a silent measure before you play.
- Always look ahead while playing, and keep your mind ahead of your hands.
- Don't stop when you make a mistake. Keep your count and place in the music.
- For continuity, practice the entire piece at a slower tempo before playing it up to speed.
- Exaggerate your dynamics as it will help to make your playing more expressive.

Great drummers have a rock-solid beat, relaxed hands, and are sensitive to balance and how they function within an ensemble. When the enclosed solos are practiced with proper consideration, students will be able to understand that dynamics can elevate an everyday drummer or percussionist into a world-class musician!

Explanation of Terms

fff **(fortississimo):** very, very loud

ff **(fortissimo):** very loud

f **(forte):** loud

mf **(mezzo forte):** moderately loud

mp **(mezzo piano):** moderately soft

p **(piano):** soft

pp **(pianissimo):** very soft

ppp **(pianississimo):** very, very soft

fp **(forte piano):** loud, then suddenly soft

> **(accent):** play the note a little louder

◁ **(crescendo):** gradually get louder

▷ **(decrescendo):** gradually get softer

Boots & Slippers

Boots & Slippers focuses on loud (forte) and soft (piano) dynamics. Keep a steady tempo and remember not to slow down when playing softly.

Knock, Knock, Who's There?

Hint: Say the name of the piece in rhythm while playing the first measure. The measure that follows will always be a response.

Right Away

Stickings can have a major impact on how we phrase. Where left-hand stickings are noted, play near the rim of the drum. Where right-hand stickings are noted, play near the center. If no stickings are indicated, play with both hands in the center.

Two Left On

For right-hand players, playing doubles (or diddles) with the left hand can be challenging. Be sure to stay relaxed, lift with the wrist, and take advantage of the generous rebound provided by the drumhead. Be alert, as the right hand has something to say at the end!

Blues in Three

Blues in Three can be counted in a slow nine at first. Once the piece is within grasp, count in a "blues-ish" side-to-side three count, subtly emphasizing the strong beats to create an inviting pulse. Where rolls are indicated, subdivide sixteenth notes and play five-stroke rolls.

Calypso Hippo

With snares off, the first four measures of this piece should be performed like a fanfare. Measure five begins with a calypso rhythm played considerably under tempo (hence the "Hippo"). You're bound to come across this rhythm again, particularly in drumset studies.

Soft-Shoe Louie

Soft shoe is a vaudeville dance performed in soft-soled shoes. In this piece, the dynamics and rhythms should be kept light and airy, as though danced. Playing with brushes can add a nice touch.

Horseplay

Because "3" is an odd number and $\frac{6}{8}$ is usually counted in two groups of 3, playing hand-to-hand in $\frac{6}{8}$ will often result in alternate hands landing on strong beats (measures 29–40). In a piece of this nature, knowing in advance which hand will play an accent or land on a strong beat is of the utmost importance. Always mark your preferred stickings over questionable accents. Even if you temporarily lose your count, clearly-marked stickings will often come to the rescue.

Double Dippo, Dancing Hippo

The use of *fp* is intended to encourage sudden, dramatic accents. In this case, however, they are a bit exaggerated due to the return of our hippo friend. Also, try to perform the "snares on" and "snares off" commands as quickly and quietly as possible while counting accurate rests.

Waltzing Brunhilda

Not known for her graceful, light-hearted ways, Brunhilda's waltz is a bit clumsy. Be free and have fun with it.

Both Sides March

"Both sides," in this context, means to play with both hands. To maximize the intended benefit of this piece, play hand-to-hand (alternate) throughout, including the rolls. Be sure not to favor your strong hand when rolling and always look ahead, particularly when approaching repeat signs!

Moderate march ♩ = 112

Grand Canyon

Grand Canyon is a study in near and distant sounds. Referencing the sound of echoes will be helpful in performing the sections marked "maestoso."

Jamtrak

Although the rolls in *Jamtrak* should be played in the closed orchestra style, measure your wrist strokes in subdivided sixteenth notes and keep your hands relaxed. Be sure not to drag the tempo while rolling and write your stickings over the accents. Remember, a pencil is a musician's best friend!

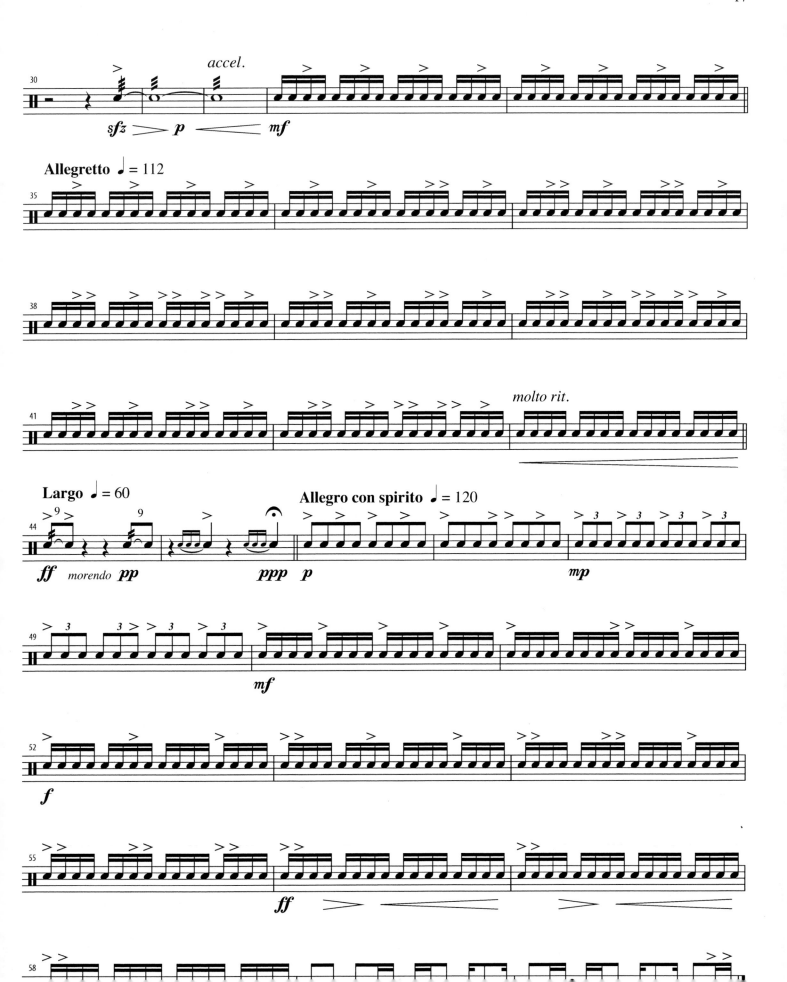

Planet Roll

Again, it can be difficult to maintain a steady tempo while rolling. If playing measured rolls (subdividing specific rhythms while rolling), make sure the subdivisions are felt but not heard. This can also be a challenge on timpani and mallet instruments as well. The dynamics in measures 32–36 may be interpreted in a couple of different ways. Determine which better suits your interpretation of the piece.

The Curious Count

Drummers and percussionists must feel comfortable in odd and fluctuating time signatures. Keep the eighth note consistent throughout. If practiced often enough, you'll not only be able to play the rhythms accurately, but perform them with a better sense of meter and purpose.

Subdivider

At slower tempos, choosing a subdivided note value to aid in counting throughout the piece is a must. Players are more prone to rushing longer note values after playing busy, subdivided phrases. In order to maintain accurate time, keep subdividing (in this case eighth notes) when playing longer note values.

Groove Trail

Marked "loosely," the rhythms in *Groove Trail* should be played in as laid back a style as possible. Take your time and lay it down.

Uncle's Ant Farm

Before playing "as fast as possible," practice the piece slowly, and gradually measure your progress with a metronome. Playing fast tempos softly for long stretches of time can be quite a challenge, as it often requires more energy to play effectively at soft dynamics. To play the 32nd notes starting in measure 53, simply continue to play 16ths and double (diddle) each side. Always look ahead when reading music, particularly when moving from line to line at fast tempos.

As fast as possible.

23

24

About the Author

Since his scholarship studies at the Juilliard School of Music, Brian has continued to pioneer innovative paths in the percussion field. Grammy-nominated as "Best New Classical Artist," Brian has appeared on NBC's *Tonight Show, Entertainment Tonight*, the *CBS Morning News*, and NPR's *All Things Considered*. Mr. Slawson's extensive discography includes solo releases on both the Sony/CBS and Belltone labels. His smash debut, *Bach on Wood*, hit Billboard's Top 10 and remains one of the world's premier vehicles for exposing new audiences to classical music.

Brian has shared the stage with classical luminaries such as Leonard Bernstein and Aaron Copland, recorded with pop icons from Stevie Ray Vaughan to Marie Osmond, and has punctuated jokes for comedians Jerry Seinfeld, Eddie Murphy, Bill Maher, and Don Rickles. He is the accessory percussionist and voice of "Gusto the Bulldog" on Warner Brothers' *Music Expressions* curriculum and a featured artist in McGraw-Hill's *Spotlight on Music*. In addition to serving as Principal Timpanist of the Brevard Symphony Orchestra, Brian's multi-media company, Slawsongs, has created award-winning custom music for feature films, television, and radio.

Mr. Slawson proudly endorses Ludwig-Musser, Zildjian, Vic Firth, Grover Pro Percussion, Rhythm Tech, Alternate Mode, and Sibelius. His teachers have included Saul Goodman, Buster Bailey, Alexander Lepak, David Smith, and Drew Grouse.

Legendary vibraphonist, Lionel Hampton, described Brian Slawson as "one of the finest percussionists to come along in many years." *Modern Drummer* magazine hails Brian as "a visionary, be it performer, producer, or composer."

Check out these other great titles in our
PERCUSSION PERFORMANCE SERIES

Classic Mallet Trios
(4 Classics Arranged for Marimba and Vibraphone)

Music by Bach, Handel, Bizet and Scarlatti
Arranged by Brian Slawson
Grade Level: 2–3 (Medium Easy to Medium) • (37479)

The Cole Porter Mallet Collection
(5 Classics Arranged for Marimba and Vibraphone)

Words and Music by Cole Porter
Arranged by Anders Åstrand
Grade Level: 3–4 (Medium to Medium Difficult) • (34213)

Concert & Recital Solos for Timpani

By Salvatore Rabbio
Grade Level: 3–4 (Medium to Medium Difficult) • (37480)

Day Rudimental Solos

By Paul Smith
Grade Level: 3 (Medium) • (34471)

Dynamic Solos for Snare Drum

By Brian Slawson
Grade Level: 1–3 (Easy to Medium) • (37481)

Fantasy on a Shona Theme
(For Solo Vibraphone or Marimba)

By Glenn Kotche
Grade Level: 3 (Medium) • (30246)

Four Rudimental Solos for Snare Drum

By Alan Keown
Grade Level: Intermediate • (30272)

The Gershwin Mallet Collection
(5 Classics Arranged for Marimba and Vibraphone)

Music by George Gershwin®
Arranged by Anders Åstrand
Grade Level: 3–4 (Medium to Medium Difficult) • (30727)

Gershwin Preludes (I–III) for Mallet Ensemble

By George Gershwin®
Arranged by Jeremy Clark
Grade Level: 3½ (Medium Difficult) • (34456)

Rhapsody in Blue
(Solo Marimba and Piano)

By George Gershwin®
Arranged by Linda Maxey
Grade Level: 5 (Difficult) • (28270)

Solos & Duets for Snare Drum

By Louie Bellson
Grade Level: 2–3 (Medium Easy to Medium) • (34470)

ISBN-10: 0-7390-8069-5
ISBN-13: 978-0-7390-8069-6

alfred.com

37481 $8.99 in

ISBN 0-7390-8069-5

9 780739 080696

0 38081 42060 8

T2-BOE-071